Steam
Juicer
Cookbook

MAKE FRESH JUICE WITH STEAM JUICER

TABLE OF CONTENTS

INTRODUCTION

Juicy, flavorful fruits and vegetables are at the heart of healthy, wholesome cooking. I'm so excited to share my favorite steamed recipes with you in this cookbook. Steaming is one of the most beneficial and straightforward cooking methods, allowing foods to retain more nutrients than other cooking methods. It's also quite versatile - you can steam fruits, vegetables, meats, fish, puddings and more with delicious results every time.

In these pages, you'll find a variety of mouthwatering steamed dishes, from juicy berry jams to succulent seafood. I've included detailed steaming times and instructions so you can easily recreate each recipe in your own kitchen. To get you started, I've also provided handy steaming charts for fruits, vegetables and proteins so you can easily look up optimal steaming times.

One of the beauties of steaming is how simple it is. All you need is a steamer basket and pot of boiling water. I find that a steam juicer gives the best results, circulating steam evenly around foods.

I hope this cookbook makes you want to start steaming as a quick, easy, and tasty way to cook. You can use these recipes to make jams and sauces to preserve the season's fruits and vegetables or to make meals quickly and easily. These tasty steamed treats are something I can't wait for you to try! Start the kettle, prepare some fresh ingredients, and let's steam!

WHAT IS A STEAM JUICER?

A steam juicer is a kitchen device used to extract juice from fruits by using steam. It typically consists of three main parts: a bottom water pan, a middle juice kettle, and a top fruit basket. Here's how it generally works:

- **Water Pan:** The bottom section is filled with water and placed on heat. The water is heated to produce steam.
- **Juice Kettle:** The middle section collects the juice extracted from the fruit. It has a spigot or tube for pouring out the collected juice.
- **Fruit Basket:** The top section holds the fruit that you want to juice. As the steam rises from the boiling water, it passes through the fruit basket, heating and softening the fruit.

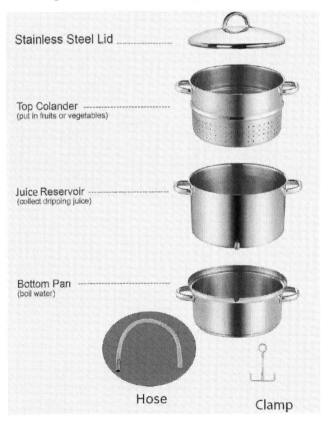

Stainless Steel Lid

Top Colander
(put in fruits or vegetables)

Juice Reservoir
(collect dripping juice)

Bottom Pan
(boil water)

Hose

Clamp

The steam causes the fruit to release its juices, which then drip down into the juice kettle. This method is particularly useful for extracting juice from high-moisture fruits like berries, grapes, or certain soft fruits.

Steam juicers are often used for making large quantities of juice, and they can be more efficient than some other methods, especially when dealing with fruits that are challenging to juice manually.

HOW TO USE A STEAM JUICER?

Using a steam juicer is a relatively straightforward process. Here's a general guide on how to use a steam juicer:

Prepare the Fruit:
- Wash and clean the fruits thoroughly.
- Remove any stems, leaves, or debris.
- It might be necessary to cut larger fruits, such as apples or pears, into smaller pieces.

Assembly:
- Set up the steam juicer by placing the bottom water pan on the stove or heat source.
- Fill the bottom pan with an appropriate amount of water. Follow the manufacturer's instructions for the recommended water level.

Add Fruits:
- Place the prepared fruits in the top fruit basket of the steam juicer.

Steam the Fruits:
- As the water in the bottom pan heats up, steam will rise through the fruit basket.
- The heat from the steam will make the fruits soft and help get the juices out of them.
- Allow the fruits to steam until they are thoroughly juiced. The duration will depend on the type and quantity of fruits you're using.

Collect the Juice:
- The juice extracted from the fruits will collect in the middle juice kettle.
- Position a container, such as a jug or bowl, under the spigot or tube of the juice kettle to collect the juice.

Monitor the Process:
- Keep an eye on the water level in the bottom pan to ensure it doesn't run dry during the juicing process.
- Adjust the heat if necessary to maintain a steady steam.

Finish and Store:
- Once the fruits are thoroughly juiced, turn off the heat and carefully remove the fruit basket.
- Let the juice cool down before putting it in containers to store.

Clean-Up:
- Clean the steam juicer thoroughly, including the fruit basket, juice kettle, and water pan, according to the manufacturer's instructions.

BENEFITS OF USING A STEAM JUICER

- **Quick Processing:** Ideal for dealing with large harvests or gifted produce.
- **Easy Preparation:** No need to peel, pit, or deseed—just wash the fruit.
- **Time-Saving:** Faster and less labor-intensive than traditional juicing methods.
- **Clean Juice:** Pulp and seeds are separated, resulting in clear concentrated juice.
- **Versatility:** Perfect for making jams, jellies, sorbet, smoothies, and more.

POTENTIAL DISADVANTAGES

- **Enzyme Impact:** Heat from steam may affect enzymes and some nutrients in the juice.
- **Caution with Heat:** Involves hot liquids and equipment, not suitable for small children or pets.
- **Accidental Burns:** Be cautious when handling hot equipment to avoid accidents.

TIPS FOR STEAM JUICING BEGINNERS

- **Secure the Hose:** Clamp the gravity-fed hose securely to avoid dripping when not in use.
- **Maintain Steam Level:** Keep the lid on to ensure the steam remains at the right level for optimal juicing.
- **Watch the Reservoir:** Avoid overflow, as precious juice could be lost, and sugar may burn.
- **Monitor Water Level:** Regularly check and replenish water in the basin to prevent scorching.
- **Utilize Leftover Pulp:** Repurpose pulp for making fruit leather or sauces.
- **Sterilize Jars:** Seal sterilized jars immediately for steam-canning and shelf-stable storage.

FRUIT STEAMING TABLE

Fruit	Steaming Time
Apples	90-120 mins
Apricots	60-90 mins
Berries (Any kind)	60-80 mins
Cherries	60 mins
Chokecherries	60 mins
Crabapples	90-120 mins
Cranberries	60 mins
Currants	60 mins
Grapes	60 mins
Peaches	60-90 mins
Pears	90-120 mins
Plums	60-90 mins
Prunes	80 mins
Rhubarb	60-90 mins
Tomatoes	60 mins

VEGETABLE STEAMING TABLE

Vegetable	Preparation	Steaming Time
Asparagus, small stalks	Cut in 2-inch length	3 mins
Asparagus, medium stalks	Cut in 2-inch length	4 mins
Asparagus, large stalks	Cut in 2-inch length	5 mins
Beans, lima small	Shelled and sorted	3 mins
Beans, lima medium	Shelled and sorted	4 mins
Beans, lima large	Shelled and sorted	5 mins
Beans, shell, green	Shelled	2 mins
Beans, snap, green or	Cut in 2-inch	4 mins

wax	length	
Broccoli	Cut in 1 1/2-inch length	5 mins
Brussels sprouts, sorted	Small size	4 mins
Brussels sprouts, sorted	Medium size	5 mins
Brussels sprouts, sorted	Large size	6 mins
Cauliflower	1-inch pieces	4 mins
Corn, whole kernel	Blanch with corn on bars, cut off after blanching	5 mins
Corn on the cob, small	Husk, wash, sort ears	8 mins
Corn on the cob, medium	Husk, wash, sort ears	10 mins
Corn on the cob, large	Husk, wash, sort ears	11 mins
Mushrooms, whole	Dip in solution of 1 teaspoon lemon juice/pint water to prevent darkening	5 mins
Mushrooms, slices	Dip in solution of 1 teaspoon lemon juice/pint water to prevent darkening	3 mins
Peas, green	Remove from pods	2.5 to 3 mins
Peppers, green or red	Wash, remove seeds, dice	2 mins
Pumpkin, seeds removed	Wash and quarter	10 mins
Squash, summer	Wash, cut into 12-inch slices	4 mins

JUICE RECIPES

1. APPLE JUICE

Total Time: 2 hours | Servings: 3-4 Quarts

Ingredients

- 10 pounds hard, ripe, juicy apples
- 1 cup sugar (optional, omit if apples are for jelly)
- 10 whole cloves
- 2 cinnamon sticks
- 4 whole allspices

Instructions

1. Wash the apples thoroughly, removing leaves or debris. You can leave them whole, but cutting them up will yield more juice.
2. If using sugar, sprinkle it over the apples. Add the cloves, cinnamon sticks, and allspice.
3. Place the apples in a steamer basket, with the spices evenly distributed. Top with the remaining apples.
4. Cover and steam over rapidly boiling water for 1 ½ to 2 hours, or until the apples have turned into a tasteless, colorless mush.
5. Extract the juice into hot sterilized bottles or jars.

6. Seal the bottles with caps or two-part lids.

2. APPLE PEAR JUICE

Total Time: 1 hour | Serving Size: 3-4 Quarts

Ingredients
- 3 pounds apples
- 3 pounds pears
- 1 to 1 1/2 cups sugar (optional)

Instructions
1. Wash the apples and pears thoroughly.
2. Cut the apples and pears into quarters or smaller pieces.
3. Place the apples and pears in the steamer juicer.
4. Turn on the steamer juicer and let it run for 45 minutes to an hour, or until the juice has stopped flowing.
5. Drain the hot juice into sterilized bottles or canning jars.
6. Seal the bottles with caps or two-part lids.

3. APPLE-ORANGE JUICE

Total Time: 1 hour | Serving Size: 1 cup

Ingredients
- 1 gallon of apples, quartered
- 1 gallon of oranges, quartered

Instructions

1. Put water in the bottom pot of your steam juicer.
2. Add the apples and oranges to the top basket of the steam juicer.
3. Cover the steam juicer and bring the water to a boil.
4. Reduce the heat to low after the water reaches a boil, then simmer the fruit juice for 45 to 60 minutes, or until tender and the juice has been extracted.
5. Remove the top basket of the steam juicer and carefully pour the juice into a large container.
6. Strain the juice through a cheesecloth-lined strainer to remove any pulp or seeds.
7. Pour the juice into clean, sterilized mason jars.

4. AMBROSIA RASPBERRY RHUBARB JUICE

Total Time: 1 hour | Serving Size: 3 Quarts

Ingredients

- 4 quarts (8 pound) fresh rhubarb, cut in 1-inch chunks
- 1-quart fresh raspberries
- 1 cup sugar

Instructions

1. Layer the rhubarb with the raspberries and sugar in the steamer basket.
2. Steam over rapidly boiling water for 60 minutes.
3. Drain the juice into hot sterilized bottles or jars.
4. Seal the bottles with caps or two-part lids.
5. Set on a rack to cool away from drafts.

5. CHERRY JUICE

Total Time: 1 hour | Serving Size: 3-4 Quarts

Ingredients

- 10 pounds tart, sweet, red, or black cherries
- 1 cup sugar (optional, omit if using juice for jelly)

Instructions

1. Wash cherries thoroughly, removing any debris.
2. Place cherries in a steamer basket.
3. If desired, sprinkle 1 cup of sugar over the cherries.
4. Cover and steam over high heat for around 1 hour.
5. Drain the hot juice into hot sterilized bottles or jars following standard directions.
6. Seal the bottles with caps or two-part lids.

6. CHOKECHERRY JUICE

Total Time: 1 hour | Serving Size: 3 1/2 Quarts

Ingredients

- 10 pounds chokecherries

Instructions

1. Wash and clean the chokecherries thoroughly.
2. Place the chokecherries in a steamer basket.
3. Steam over high heat for 1 hour.
4. Drain the hot juice into sterilized hot bottles or canning jars following standard directions.
5. Seal the bottles with caps or two-part lids.

7. CINNAMON CRANBERRY JUICE

Total Time: 1 hour | Serving Size: 3-4 Quarts

Ingredients

- 6 pounds cranberries
- 2 sticks cinnamon
- 1 to 1 1/2 cups sugar (optional; do not add if using juice for jelly)

Instructions
1. Wash cranberries thoroughly.
2. Place cranberries, cinnamon sticks, and sugar (if using) in the steamer kettle.
3. Steam over high heat for 1 hour.
4. Drain the hot juice into sterilized bottles or canning jars.
5. Seal the bottles with caps or two-part lids.

8. CRABAPPLE JUICE

Total Time: 2 hours | Serving Size: 3-4 Quarts

Ingredients
- 10 pounds crabapples
- Water for steaming

Instructions
1. Wash crabapples thoroughly, removing leaves and debris.
2. Place crabapples in a steamer basket.
3. Over rapid boiling water, cover and steam for 2 hours. Ensure the water pan is consistently filled.
4. Check the pulp remaining in the basket; it should be colorless and almost tasteless.
5. Drain off the hot juice into hot sterilized bottles or jars.
6. Top with sterilized, hot bottle caps or lids.

9. CRANBERRY APPLE JUICE

Total Time: 1 hour | Serving Size: 3-4 Quarts

Ingredients
- 3 pounds cranberries
- 3 pounds apples
- 1 to 1 1/2 cups sugar (optional)

Instructions

1. Wash cranberries and apples thoroughly.
2. Combine cranberries and apple, and sugar (if using) in the steamer basket.
3. Steam over high heat for 1 hour.
4. Drain the hot juice into sterilized bottles or canning jars.
5. Seal the bottles with caps or two-part lids.

10. CRANBERRY GRAPE JUICE

Total Time: 1 hour | Serving Size: 3-4 Quarts

Ingredients

- 3 pounds cranberries
- 3 pounds grapes (any variety), washed and stems removed
- 1 to 1 1/2 cups sugar (optional)

Instructions

1. Wash cranberries and grapes thoroughly.
2. Combine cranberries grapes and sugar in the steamer basket.
3. Steam over high heat for 1 hour, ensuring all juice is extracted from the fruit for an even blend.
4. Drain the hot juice into sterilized bottles or canning jars.
5. Seal the bottles with caps or two-part lids.

11. CURRANT AND RASPBERRY JUICE

Total Time: 1 hour | Serving Size: 4 Quarts

Ingredients

- 3 quarts fresh raspberries
- 3 quarts fresh red currants
- 2 cups sugar

Instructions

1. Clean the berries, removing any debris.
2. Layer the raspberries, currants, and sugar in the steamer basket.
3. Steam for 60 minutes over rapidly boiling water.
4. Drain the juice into hot sterilized bottles or jars.
5. Seal the bottles with caps or two-part lids.
6. Cool on a rack in a draft-free place.

12. ELDERBERRY JUICE

Total time: 1 hour | Serving size: 2 quarts

Ingredients

- 2 gallons (7.5 liters) elderberries, fresh or frozen
- 3/4-gallon (2.8 liters) water

Instructions

1. If using fresh elderberries, remove the stems. You can do this easily by freezing the elderberries for a few hours, then rubbing the stems between your gloved fingers.
2. Add the elderberries to the colander of the steam juicer.
3. Fill the water pan with water and place it on the stove over medium heat.
4. Place the colander of elderberries on top of the water pan and cover with the lid.
5. Now, bring water to a boil and reduce the heat to low and let simmer for around 30 minutes, or until the elderberries are soft and juicy.
6. Remove the steam juicer from the heat and let it cool for a few minutes.
7. Carefully remove the colander of elderberries and place it over a bowl.
8. Use a spoon to press down on the elderberries to extract the juice.
9. Transfer the juice to a clean container.

13. GRAPE JUICE

Total Time: 1 hour | Serving Size: 2 Quarts

Ingredients
- 5 1/2 pounds ripe grapes

Instructions
1. Place the cleaned grapes in the steamer basket.
2. Steam over high heat about 1 hour or until grapes are colorless and dry.
3. Drain the hot juice into sterilized bottles or canning jars.
4. Seal the bottles with caps or two-part lids.
5. Let cool on a rack set in a draft-free place.

14. MINT ESSENCE

Total Time: 1 hour | Serving Size: 4-5 Quarts

Ingredients
- 3 quarts mint leaves
- 1 cup sugar

Instructions
1. Wash mint leaves thoroughly.
2. Place the mint leaves into a steamer basket, ensuring not to pack them tightly. Let the leaves fluff up in the basket.
3. Steam the mint leaves for 1 hour over rapidly boiling water.
4. Drain the extracted essence out of the basket into sterilized jars.

5. Seal the jars securely.

15. PEACH AND RASPBERRY JUICE

Total Time: 1.30 hours | Serving Size: 2 Quarts

Ingredients
- 2.5 pounds fresh ripe peaches, halved and pitted
- 2.5 pounds fresh raspberries
- 1 cup sugar (optional)

Instructions
1. Combine halved and pitted peaches with fresh raspberries.
2. Place the mixed fruit in the steamer basket.
3. Steam over high heat for 1 1/2 hours or until the peaches look "drained" and dry.
4. If desired, sprinkle sugar over the fruit during steaming.
5. Drain the hot juice into sterilized bottles or hot canning jars.
6. Seal the bottles with caps or two-part lids.
7. Let cool on a rack set in a draft-free place.

16. PEACH JUICE

Total Time: 1.30 to 2 hours | Serving Size: 2 1/2 Quarts

Ingredients
- 6 pounds fresh ripe pears
- 2 cups sugar

Instructions
1. Cut washed pears in half and place them in the steamer basket.

2. Steam over high heat for 1 1/2 to 2 hours (check to be sure water doesn't boil out of the pan).
3. Pears will look drained and dry during steaming.
4. Drain the hot juice into sterilized bottles or hot canning jars.
5. Seal the bottles with caps or two-part lids.
6. Let cool on a rack set in a draft-free place.

17. PEAR JUICE

Total Time: 1.30 to 2 hours | Serving Size: 2 1/2 Quarts

Ingredients
- 6 pounds fresh ripe pears
- 2 cups sugar

Instructions
1. Cut washed pears in half and place them in the steamer basket.
2. Steam over high heat for 1 1/2 to 2 hours (check to be sure water doesn't boil out of the pan).
3. Pears will look drained and dry during steaming.
4. Drain the hot juice into sterilized bottles or hot canning jars.
5. Seal the bottles with caps or two-part lids.
6. Let cool on a rack set in a draft-free place.

18. PLUM JUICE

Total Time: 1 to 1.30 hours | Serving Size: 4 Quarts

Ingredients
- 10 pounds wild, blue, or prune plums
- 1 cup sugar (optional, omit if juice is for jelly)

21

Instructions

1. Layer the cleaned plums (it isn't necessary to pit and halve if the plums are little wild ones) in the steamer basket.
2. If using sugar, sprinkle it over the plums.
3. Steam over high heat for about 1 to 1 1/2 hours or until plums look dry.
4. Drain the hot juice into sterilized bottles or jars.
5. Seal the bottles with caps or two-part lids.

19. CURRANT JUICE

Total Time: 1 hour | Serving Size: 5 Quarts

Ingredients

- 6 quarts fresh red currants
- 2 cups sugar

Instructions

1. Place fresh red currants and sugar in a steamer basket.
2. Layer the currants and sugar evenly.
3. Steam the currants over rapidly boiling water for 60 minutes.
4. Once steamed, drain the juice into hot sterilized bottles or jars.
5. Top the bottles or jars with hot bottle caps or two-part lids.
6. Allow the juice to cool on a rack in a draft-free place.

20. RHUBARB JUICE

Total Time: 1 to 1.30 hours | Serving Size: 2 Quarts

Ingredients

- 5 quarts rhubarb, cut up, unpeeled
- 3 cups sugar

Instructions

1. Layer the cut-up rhubarb with sugar in the perforated steaming basket.
2. Cover and place the basket over a water pan filled with boiling water to about 1 1/2 inches from the top.
3. Steam for around 1 to 1 1/2 hours or until the rhubarb appears limp, colorless, and "dry."
4. Have hot sterilized bottles or jars ready (hold them in a 200°F oven if desired), and prepare bottle caps or lids by keeping them in boiling water.
5. Extract the juice into the prepared bottles or jars.
6. Put the cap or lid on immediately and let cool on a rack in a draft-free place.

21. RASPBERRY JUICE

Total Time: 1 hour | Serving Size: 3 Quarts

Ingredients

- 8 pounds (4 quarts) fresh raspberries, cleaned
- 1 1/2 cups sugar

Instructions

1. Layer two quarts of the raspberries in the perforated steaming basket.
2. Sprinkle half of the sugar over the first layer of raspberries, then add the remaining two quarts of berries.
3. Sprinkle the second half of the sugar over the top layer of raspberries.
4. Cover and set over a water pan filled to about 1 and 1/2 inches from the top; bring to a rapid boil.
5. Steam the berries for 45 minutes to 1 hour or until they look "faded."
6. Have hot sterilized bottles or jars ready; hold jars or bottles in an oven set at 200°F.
7. Keep the bottle caps or lids in boiling water in a small pan.
8. Extract the juice through the rubber tube into hot bottles or jars.
9. Cap immediately and let cool on a rack or folded piece of cloth, well apart, away from drafts.

22. RHUBARB AND GINGER JUICE

Total Time: 1 hour | Serving Size: Variable

Ingredients

- **For juice:** 150 - 250g / 5½ - 9 oz per one kilo of rhubarb; **For cordial:** 500 - 650g / 18 - 23 oz per one kilo of rhubarb
- Fresh Ginger Root – 100 - 200g / 3½ - 7 oz peeled finely sliced, grated or shredded
- Granulated sugar according to taste- layered with the fruit;
- Freshly gathered Rhubarb stalks, washed, drained & cut into small pieces

Instructions

1. Put water in the steam juice extractor's base pan as the manufacturer has instructed. Then, put the juice collection pot and the steamer basket on top of the water.
2. In the steamer basket, layer the rhubarb, sugar, and shredded ginger in that order.
3. Put it in the steam for about 45 minutes.
4. Once the first juice has gathered in the collection pot, strain it into a jug and then pour it back over the fruit in the steaming basket. This helps the sugar get distributed evenly in the juice.
5. When the process is done, pour the liquid into hot screw-top bottles, tighten the lid, and turn the bottle upside down. This heats the cap and makes it pasteurized. Let the liquid cool.

6. Keep it in a dark place to keep the color fresh.
7. Juice that has been opened should be kept in the fridge and drunk within three days. As cordial has more sugar than juice, it will last for a few weeks after it has been opened.

23. STRAWBERRY JUICE

Total Time: 1 hour | Serving Size: 3 1/2 Quarts

Ingredients

- 4 quarts strawberries, washed, stems removed
- 1 cup sugar (2 cups if strawberries are very tart)

Instructions

1. Layer two quarts of strawberries into the perforated steaming basket.
2. Sprinkle half of the sugar over the first layer of strawberries.
3. Top with the remaining two quarts of strawberries and the remaining sugar.
4. Put the cover on and set over a water pan with water to about 1 1/2 inches from the top of the pan, at a rapid boil.
5. Steam for 45 minutes to 1 hour.
6. Have hot sterilized bottles or jars ready.
7. Drain the hot juice into bottles or jars.
8. Seal the bottles with caps or two-part lids.

24. STRAWBERRY RHUBARB JUICE

Total Time: 1 hour | Serving Size: 4-5 Quarts

Ingredients

- 3 quarts strawberries
- 3 quarts rhubarb, cut into one-inch cubes
- 2 cups sugar

Instructions

1. Clean berries, removing any debris.
2. Layer strawberries, rhubarb, and sugar in the steamer basket.
3. Steam for 60 minutes.
4. Drain the juice into hot sterilized bottles or jars.
5. Top with hot Mehu-Maija bottle caps or two-part lids.
6. Cool on a rack in a draft-free place.

25. BASIC JELLY

Total Time: 20 minutes | Serving Size: About four half-pints of jelly

Ingredients

- 4 cups juice
- Sugar: 4 cups if juice has high pectin, 3 cups if medium pectin, 2 cups if low pectin

Instructions

1. Bring juice to a boil in a large enamel or stainless-steel pan.
2. Simmer for about 5 minutes, then skim off any impurities.
3. Add the measured sugar and stir until dissolved. Keep the juice at a simmer to protect pectin and color.
4. Stop stirring and let it simmer for about 10 minutes.
5. To test for the jelly stage, place a small amount of the mixture on a spoon and let it drop back into the pan. It's ready when the mixture forms a sheet on the spoon and divides into two big drops. If using a candy thermometer, it should register 220 to 222°F.
6. Meanwhile, keep jelly jars and lids in boiling water. Remove just before needed, drain, and let dry by inverting on a rack.
7. Leave about 1/4 inch of space at the top of the jars after filling them with hot jelly.
8. Seal the jars with paraffin or two-part lids.
9. Before serving, allow the jelly to cool and solidify.

STEAMED MEAT

26. STEAMED CHICKEN

Total Time: 3 hours | Serving Size: 4-6

Ingredients

- 1 stewing or roasting chicken, disjointed or left whole
- Parsley
- Paprika
- 1 Carrots
- 1 Potatoes
- Broccoli or Cauliflower

Instructions

1. Place the washed and dried roasting chicken in the steamer basket.
2. Sprinkle with parsley and paprika for added flavor.
3. Cover and steam with water at a simmer (no hotter than 185°F) for 2 to 2.5 hours or until chicken is tender when pierced with a fork.
4. About 30 minutes before the chicken is done, add whole carrots, potatoes, broccoli or cauliflower to the pot.
5. If the vegetables are still not done when the chicken is done, take the chicken out, raise the heat, and steam for another 5 to 10 minutes.
6. Drippings from the chicken, along with condensed water, can be boiled down, seasoned, and thickened to make a delicious gravy.

27. CORNED BEEF AND CABBAGE

Total Time: 2 hours | Serving Size: 4-6

Ingredients

- 1 corned beef (prepared as directed for chicken)
- 1 to 4 teaspoons caraway seeds (optional)
- Cabbage, cut into wedges

Instructions

1. Place the beef in the steamer basket.
2. Sprinkle with parsley and paprika for added flavor.
3. If desired, season the corned beef with 1 to 4 teaspoons of caraway seeds.
4. Cover the corned beef and steam it with water that is barely simmering (no hotter than 185°F) for about an hour and a half to two hours, or until a fork can go through it easily.
5. About 30 minutes before the corned beef is done, add cabbage wedges to the pot.
6. If the cabbage isn't done when the corned beef is ready, remove the corned beef, turn up the heat, and steam for an additional 5 to 10 minutes.
7. Collect drippings from the corned beef, along with condensed water. Boil down, season, and thicken to create a flavorful gravy.

28. STEAMED HAM

Total Time: 30 mins | Serving Size: 4-6

Ingredients
- 1 ham (large or small)
- Parsley
- Paprika

Instructions
1. Place the washed and dried ham in the steamer basket.
2. Sprinkle with parsley and paprika for enhanced flavor.
3. Cover and steam with water at a simmer (no hotter than 185°F) for the recommended time based on ham size (20 mins per pound for a large ham, and 30 mins for small one), ensuring it is cooked thoroughly.
4. Boil down the drippings from the ham to make a savory gravy.
5. Optionally, save the drippings for adding to pea or bean soup for added flavor.

29. MEAT SAUSAGE

Total Time: 1 hour 50 mins | Serving Size: 2.5 Quarts

Ingredients

- 5 pounds of hamburger meat
- 2 tablespoons salt
- 2 tablespoons salt
- 2 1/2 teaspoons of coarsely ground black pepper
- 1 teaspoon hickory smoke salt
- 2 1/2 teaspoons whole mustard seed
- 2 1/2 teaspoons garlic salt
- 1/2 teaspoon saltpeter (optional; for reddish color)

Instructions

1. Take a large bowl and mix all ingredients thoroughly.
2. Refrigerate the mixture for around 8 to 12 hours to allow flavors to blend.
3. Shape the mixture into 4 rolls of uniform size and shape.
4. Wrap each roll in aluminum foil.
5. Place the foil-wrapped rolls in a steamer basket.
6. Steam over vigorously boiling water for 1 hour and 15 minutes.
7. Remove from the steamer and chill immediately.
8. Once chilled, slice the sausage rolls thinly.
9. Enjoy your homemade sausage!

30. VEGETABLE BROTH

Total time: 1 hour | Serving size: 1 gallon of broth and 1 jar of powdered bouillon

Ingredients

- 1 gallon of vegetable scraps (frozen or fresh)

Instructions

1. Place the vegetable scraps in the bottom of a steam juicer.
2. Add water to the steam juicer's base, just enough to cover the scraps, but no more than one inch.
3. Place the cover on the steam juicer and bring the water to a boil.
4. While the water is still boiling, turn down the heat and let the vegetables steam for one hour.
5. Remove the cover from the steam juicer and carefully pour the broth into a jar.
6. Let the broth cool completely. Once the broth is cool, you can either use it immediately or freeze it for later.

STEAMED FISH AND SEAFOOD

31. STEAMED FISH

Total Time: 15 minutes | Serving Size: 4 servings

Ingredients

- 2 lbs. fresh fish fillets (cut if thicker than 2 inches)
- Lemon juice
- Fresh chopped parsley
- Melted butter

Instructions

1. Cut fish if more than 2 inches thick, ensuring uniform thickness. Place fish into a steamer basket.

2. Cover and steam for around 10 minutes, or you need to wait until the fish flakes easily with a fork.
3. Serve hot, drizzled with lemon juice.
4. Garnish with fresh chopped parsley. Optionally, serve with melted butter on the side.

32. STEAMED LOBSTER

Total Time: 12-15 minutes | Serving Size: 2

Ingredients
- 2 lobsters, cleaned and washed
- Lemon wedges
- Melted butter for dipping

Instructions
1. Thoroughly wash the lobsters.
2. Place the lobsters in a steamer basket.
3. Bring water to a high boil in a pot.
4. Steam the lobsters over high heat for 10 to 12 minutes.
5. Remove from the steamer and let them cool slightly.
6. Now, you can serve it with lemon wedges and melted butter for dipping.

33. STEAMED CRABS

Total Time: 8-10 minutes | Serving Size: 4 servings

Ingredients
- Fresh crabs

Instructions
1. Wash crabs thoroughly.
2. Place crabs in a steamer basket.
3. Steam over high heat for around 8 to 10 minutes.
4. Serve with a side of lemon juice and melted butter.

34. STEAMED CRAWFISH

Total Time: 5-6 minutes | Serving Size: 4

Ingredients
- 2 pounds of fresh crawfish
- Lemon wedges
- Melted butter

Instructions
1. Wash crawfish thoroughly.
2. Place crawfish in a steamer basket.
3. Steam over high boil for 5-6 minutes.
4. Shellfish continue to cook as they cool.
5. Serve steamed crawfish with lemon wedges and melted butter.

35. STEAMED SHRIMPS

Total Time: 3-5 minutes | Serving Size: 4

Ingredients
- 1-pound fresh shrimp, shells intact

Instructions
1. Wash the shrimps thoroughly.
2. Place the shrimps in a steamer basket without removing the shells.
3. Steam over boiling water for 3 to 5 minutes or until the shrimps turn pink. Be cautious not to overcook.
4. Smaller shrimps will cook faster than larger pieces. Ensure they are thoroughly cooked before removing from heat.
5. Remove from heat and carefully take off the lid.

36. STEAMED CLAMS

Total Time: 3-5 minutes | Serving Size: Depends on ingredients

Ingredients

- Fresh clams

Instructions

1. Wash the clams thoroughly.
2. Place the clams in a steamer basket without removing the shells.
3. Bring water to a boil in a steamer.
4. Steam the clams over boiling water for 3 to 5 minutes or until they are done. Be cautious not to overcook.
5. Smaller clams will cook faster than larger ones, so check for doneness before removing from heat.
6. Remove from heat and take off the lid.

37. STEAMED MUSSELS

Total Time: 3-5 minutes | Serving Size: Variable

Ingredients

- Fresh mussels

Instructions

1. Wash mussels thoroughly.
2. Place mussels in a steamer basket, leaving shells intact.
3. Steam over boiling water for 3 to 5 minutes or until mussels are done.
4. Be cautious not to overcook; smaller pieces cook faster than larger ones.
5. Check for doneness before removing from heat.
6. Remove from heat, take off the lid, and enjoy!

PUDDING

38. STEAMED PUMPKIN PUDDING

Total Time: 2 hours 5 minutes | Serving Size: 10-12 servings

Ingredients

- 3/4 cup canned or cooked and mashed pumpkin
- 1 cup firmly packed brown sugar
- 1/2 cup shortening (part butter)
- 3/4 cup chopped pecans or walnuts
- 1 teaspoon salt
- 1/4 cup sour cream or light cream
- 2 eggs, beaten
- 1/4 cup white sugar
- 2 cups sifted all-purpose flour
- 1/4 teaspoon ginger
- 1 1/2 teaspoons baking powder
- 1/4 teaspoon baking soda
- 1 teaspoon pumpkin pie spice

Instructions

1. Cream the shortening with brown sugar and white sugar; add salt, pumpkin pie spice, ginger, and beaten eggs. Beat well.
2. Stir in chopped nuts.
3. Now, sift flour with baking powder and soda, then you need to add to the creamed mixture alternately with pumpkin and sour cream or light cream. Mix well after each addition.
4. Turn batter into a well-greased 2-quart mold and cover the top tightly.
5. Set the mold in a steamer basket and steam over continuously boiling water for 2 hours.
6. Let stand for 5 minutes before removing from the mold.

39. STEAMED CARROT PUDDING

Total Time: 3 hours (large mold) or 1.5 hours (individual molds) | Serving Size: 8

Ingredients

- 1 cup fine dry bread crumbs
- 2 eggs, slightly beaten
- 1 cup finely shredded raw carrots
- 1 teaspoon allspice
- 1 cup ground raisins
- 1 tablespoon dark molasses
- 1 teaspoon nutmeg
- 1 cup ground suet
- 1 teaspoon soda
- 1 cup chopped walnuts
- 1 cup brown sugar
- 1/2 teaspoon salt
- 1/2 teaspoon cloves
- 1 cup shredded raw potatoes
- 1 teaspoon cinnamon
- 1 cup all-purpose flour

Instructions

1. First, you need to Sift flour, measure, and sift again with soda, cinnamon, nutmeg, allspice, cloves, and salt into a bowl.
2. Stir in bread crumbs, brown sugar, carrots, potatoes, raisins, walnuts, and suet until ingredients are blended and moistened.
3. Mix in molasses and eggs until blended.
4. Turn the mixture into a buttered 2-quart pudding mold (or 8 individual molds).
5. Place in steamer basket over continuously boiling water.
6. Cover and steam for 3 hours (large mold) or 1.5 hours (individual molds). Ensure the steamer doesn't run dry.
7. Remove molds from steamer, cool for 10 minutes, then remove from mold.

8. Serve hot or wrap when cold for storage and freezing.
9. Serve with brown sugar sauce.

40. STEAMED PLUM PUDDING

Total Time: 6 hours | Serving Size: 8-10 servings

Ingredients
- 1/4 cup fruit juice, brandy, or sherry
- 1 cup brown sugar
- 3/4 teaspoon mace
- 2 cups ground suet (about 1/2 pound)
- 11/2 cups cut raisins
- 1 teaspoon ground cinnamon
- 11/2 cups coarse soft bread crumbs
- 3/4 cup chopped walnuts
- 3/4 cup finely cut citron
- 1 teaspoon salt
- 3/4 cup candied lemon peel
- 1 teaspoon baking soda
- 11/2 cups currants
- 1 cup sifted all-purpose flour
- 3 eggs, beaten
- 3/4 cup candied orange peel
- 1/4 teaspoon nutmeg
- 6 tablespoons currant jelly

Instructions
1. First, put all-purpose flour, salt, baking soda, and spices in a large bowl and sift them together.
2. Mix in raisins, currants, citron, candied orange peel, candied lemon peel, walnuts, and bread crumbs.
3. In a separate bowl, combine suet, brown sugar, beaten eggs, currant jelly, and fruit juice or brandy. Blend well.
4. Add the wet mixture to the fruit mixture, stirring thoroughly.
5. Pour the combined mixture into a well-greased 2-quart mold.
6. Steam over continuously boiling water for 6 hours.

7. Remove from the mold, soak in brandy, wrap well, and age for at least 4 weeks.

The End.

Made in United States
Troutdale, OR
09/17/2024

22883208R00022